CW01497073

Introduction to Economics
by Robert Jameson

Copyright 2013 Robert Jameson

Warning/Disclaimer

This book shouldn't offend anyone - but, with so many ridiculously over-sensitive people around these days, there's always a danger that it will. Please note, therefore, that you read this book at your own risk. Furthermore, please note that this is a book of ideas and that none of the contents of this book are intended to be read as statements of fact.

Contents

Introduction

This book is intended for students who are considering studying Economics, for students who are soon to begin a course in Economics and for those who are already studying Economics but who would like to firm up their understanding of some of the key principles. It doesn't particularly matter if you are still at school or if you are about to begin a college or university course.

This book is intended to give you a head start on understanding a whole bunch of core Economics concepts - and thus give you a sure, firm foundation in the great and fascinating discipline that is Economics.

This is not designed to be a comprehensive set of key concepts. It is not a textbook. The concepts included here are merely a selection which I hope will give you an opportunity to learn to see things through an economist's eyes - and get a feel for the special way a real economist understands the world.

Economics is an incredibly useful discipline and a skilled economist is someone who, if they're listened to, can be of enormous value to governments, businesses and individuals. So many of the problems we face as individuals and as a society would be much easier to solve if we were prepared to listen to the advice of skilled economists.

The trouble is that very few people actually understand Economics. There are a lot of people who think they understand it or pretend to understand it, but they rarely do. Even many of the people who have Economics qualifications and many of the people with 'Economist' in their job title, have a very poor understanding of what Economics is actually all about. And, if you pay attention to the news at all, you might have begun to develop the nagging suspicion that the politicians who are supposed to be in charge of running our economy don't have a clue about Economics either!

Many people just don't 'get' Economics. Some people 'get it' almost straight away - but far more people never get it at all, even having studied it for years. They somehow get confused and never really grasp the fundamental concepts and principles at the very core of the subject.

It can often be the case that, when people study for an Economics qualification, they quickly become embroiled in learning terms, drawing diagrams and answering questions on topical case studies. Before they know it, they're preparing for exams by studying marking schemes and developing their exam techniques. Somewhere along the way, they've skipped over and failed to properly understand the fundamental concepts and principles that everything else is supposed to be based upon.

This failure to understand important concepts manifests itself in various, seemingly minor errors in your work. Individually, these errors may be easy to correct - but it can be very difficult, later on, with exams approaching, to find the time to correct the fundamental misunderstandings that led to those seemingly minor errors.

Further errors will occur - and these might possibly knock you down a grade or two - but the really big problem is that you don't understand Economics. If you're ever supposed to advise someone - a government, a business or an individual - on an

Economics matter, you'll just be faking it. You won't really understand what you're talking about. You won't be able to use your abilities as a skilled economist to help your country, your employer or your own mother, because you won't *be* a skilled economist. You'll just be another 'bullshitter' (and yes, that is the appropriate technical term!) - and, seriously now, we don't need any more of those as we have more than enough already!

So - this book is about avoiding all that aggro of living a life as a lowlife bullshitter who doesn't really know what they're talking about. I'm fed up with turning on the news to see fake economists pretending they understand Economics. I'm fed up with politicians who are supposed to be running the country, yet don't have a clue about some of the most basic and fundamental Economics concepts that they really need to know about in order to do their jobs properly. I'd like to see a future where this sort of thing doesn't happen quite so often.

There are lots of people who pretend to understand Economics, but there are very few who really do understand Economics. If you dive into Economics and race towards your exams without taking the time to properly understand the key concepts at the heart of the subject, it will hardly be a surprise if you end up amongst the fakers rather than amongst the true experts.

A Special Calling

As you develop your skills as an economist, you may develop the tendency to become a complete snob about all the courses in 'lesser subjects' - such as Business, Management or Accountancy - that don't compare to a 'proper' Economics course. This is one type of snobbery that I would like to vehemently encourage!

Economics is a proper subject. It is a proper academic discipline. It's got real meat and guts to it. It's got concepts and ideas. It's not about trendy business terms and farcical management-speak - these are the tools that bullshitters use to hide their incompetence and lack of understanding. Proper economists don't need these things. Plain English is our preferred method of communication. Yes, we have specialist terms, but they're real terms, with proper meanings to them. They're there to communicate important concepts, not mask our ineptitude.

There are lots of business-types, management-types, finance-types and accountancy-obsessives around. Too many, in fact! Some of them fool themselves into thinking they understand something about Economics, but we proper economists look down on many such people - and so we should! Most of them don't have a clue!

Make no mistake - Economics is a much bigger, much more important and much more interesting subject than 'Business' or 'Management' or 'Accountancy' or 'Marketing.'

Economics is a very special calling. The resource considerations of the human species are about much more than just making a profit, growing a business and balancing the books. We are the species that has been able to count Da Vinci, Mozart, Einstein, Shakespeare, Jung, Attlee and Socrates amongst our number. We've been to the moon. We've begun to unravel the secrets of genetics. We've grappled with the great questions of existence. If you're only interested in balancing the books for some poxy advertising agency or brainwashing children into buying your sugary drinks, then perhaps you should go and amuse yourself elsewhere!

Real economists care about a great many important things. We care about all the people in the world who don't have enough to eat. We care about people who never have a proper childhood when they can play, explore and develop their interests. We care about people who don't receive a decent education. We care about people who don't get many opportunities in life because their parents weren't very wealthy or well-educated or because they live in a very unstable country.

We care about people who find it difficult to get a job or whose ambitions are thwarted by government taxes and regulations. We care about people who have to work long hours for low wages and don't get a reasonable amount of leisure time to spend with their families. We care about people who have to work into their old age because they can't afford to retire.

We care about conservation and wonder how we can meet mankind's needs without destroying the planet we live on. We care about how we can find the resources we need to explore the universe we live in and make important discoveries. We care about science, technology, art, culture and the general advancement of society.

If you don't care about all or at least most of these

things, then .... (How can I put this politely?) ......
well, then perhaps Economics just isn't for you!

Money and Resources

Before you can learn what Economics is, it is really going to help if you can first clear your mind of some of the common, but fundamentally misleading misconceptions about what Economics is actually about.

The biggest misconception about Economics concerns money. This would come as quite a surprise to most of the population, but Economics is *not* about money. Most people seem to think it is, but it isn't! Just take a deep breath and bear with me on this one - I'm an expert!

Think of it like this: We use money to buy food, housing, books and thousands of other goods and services. The money goes one way (to the person or business we buy those goods from) and the food, housing and books go the other way (to us, the consumers of those goods) - but it's the food, housing and books that are the really important things. If these important resources continued to be supplied, but no money changed hands, we'd be OK - we could carry on as before. On the other hand, if money moved, but no resources were supplied, we'd all starve to death. That's the difference in importance between money and real resources!

Money is relatively unimportant. We can survive without money. This, after all, is exactly what the human race did for many thousands of years. Instead of using money, early man simply used a system of bartering - people would simply swap things they had plenty of for other things they didn't produce themselves. Many people didn't even use bartering. They simply met all their needs for themselves, by harvesting the bounty of the natural world around them.

Money is very useful, of course, as it allows much more complex trading than would be possible with only a bartering system. However, this doesn't make it more important than the actual resources we need to survive. We can survive without money, but we cannot survive without real resources.

Furthermore, as a species, if we had less money, this needn't make us any worse off at all. Imagine that tomorrow, as if by magic, half the money in the world simply disappeared. Every individual person looked in their wallets, purses, under their mattresses and in their bank accounts - and found that half their money was missing.

This would undoubtedly cause a lot of head scratching. However, it is not a disaster. Although we'd all have less money than before, we wouldn't have lost any of our real resources. We'd still have the same number of farms, people, houses, cars and factories as before. If you think about it, all we'd need to do would be to cut the prices of everything in half, and we'd be able to carry on pretty much exactly as before.

Yet, turn on the news almost any day of the year and you could easily get the impression that all the world's economic problems are due to a lack of money. Politicians or commentators might argue that we can't afford to build new schools or provide better healthcare because we don't have enough money. They might claim that we don't have enough money to provide everyone with a decent pension and a comfortable retirement at a reasonable age. Such claims, however, are nonsense! They're complete fiction!

If lack of money really was at the heart of all our

economic problems, we could simply print more of it. Our governments are never actually going to literally run out of money. They have the legal right and the facilities to print as much money as they could ever possibly want or need.

Of course, simply printing loads of money wouldn't actually solve our economic problems - but that's because lack of money isn't the cause of our problems in the first place. Printing money might only cause prices to go up - and that's because, whilst we can pretty much magic more money up out of thin air, we can't magic real resources out of thin air.

Economics is not really about money. It's about real people, real resources and real achievements. It's about looking at how we, the people who live on this planet, use the real resources available to us and how we can organise ourselves more effectively so that we can make better use of those resources and achieve more as a result.

Sometimes, we genuinely lack the necessary natural resources to get an important job done. More often than not, however, we only lack resources because we have squandered them. We've failed to make proper use of the natural resources available to us. We've wasted them. We've failed to organise ourselves effectively. These are the problems we really ought to be dealing with.

Unfortunately, with politicians and commentators in the media banging on endlessly about a lack of money, a sort of brainwashing effect takes place and both these people and the general public come to believe that movements of money are actually more important than the movements of real resources - as if the money paid for food is more important than the food itself and the people who eat it, and as if the money paid for books is of greater economic value that the education those books can provide.

It is this ridiculous and misleading assumption about the overriding importance of money that prevents people from understanding Economics. Far from economists being obsessed with money, it is the ability to see the world in terms of real resources and real people, rather than in terms of money, that is the hallmark of a real economist. You must purge your brain of this obsession with money if you are ever to be a skilled economist.

Unfortunately, most people seem incapable of doing this. They've been brainwashed for so long, it's become almost hard-wired into their brains to assume that economic difficulties are always the result of a lack of money. It doesn't matter how carefully you explain to them why this is clearly nonsense, they refuse to accept that it is. (I hope you're not one of these people!)

It is important to realise that misplaced 'money-think' crops up all over the place and gets in the way of us, as a society, identifying the causes and finding the solutions to our economic problems. You'll be reading an article by a newspaper columnist or listening to a politician on the radio. They might even seem to be making some sort of sense, as if they actually understand the issue in question. Then they'll go and blow it all by making some ridiculous remark about the country's economic problems being due to a lack of money. Why don't they just round off by claiming the moon is made of cheese?

People

Far from being about money, Economics is very much about people. In fact, it might very well be viewed as a branch of psychology. The decisions people make, the way people make decisions, the motivations behind their decisions and the factors and influences that affect their decisions - all these matters are fundamental to Economics.

It is sometimes said that Economics is the study of humans in the everyday business of life. It's about how humans go about meeting their needs and pursuing their desires and ambitions. Another useful definition is that Economics is the study of human behaviour in relation to the use and allocation of resources. These are not universally-accepted definitions, but think about it and you'll realise that there's a great deal of psychology involved in pretty much everything Economics gets involved in.

What is the market price of a house? Well, ultimately that depends upon the decisions made by individual humans. It depends on the decision made by the owner as to how much they are prepared to sell it for. It depends on the decisions made by prospective buyers as to how much they are prepared to pay for the house in question. It depends on decisions made by bank managers as to how much they are prepared to lend to the prospective buyers.

Revenues, profits, production levels, advances in technology, inflation rates, GDP, tax receipts, demand, educational standards - these all depend on the cumulative effects of decisions made by millions of individuals. The state of the markets, the state of the nation and the state of the human species as a whole depend rather precariously on the decisions of millions of individual human beings.

When studying how people behave and trying to predict the future, it is important for economists to remember that humans are not entirely rational creatures. The question of how rational or irrational people are is at the heart of many issues in Economics. Sometimes, people follow clear, logical patterns of behaviour, but they also have the capacity to be irrational and illogical. Humans, as we know, can be moody and sulky, flippant, irresponsible and reckless.

The failure to understand that Economics is fundamentally about human psychology, is at the heart of people's misunderstandings about Economics.

Economics is a science, but economic choices and thus economic theories are always at the mercy of human psychology. People change. Human beings are capable of changing, adjusting and adapting. That's why we're such a successful species! This also means, however, that Economic theories can sometimes have a limited shelf-life.

For a time, people may behave in a predictable way and, consequently, a particular economic theory may prove useful for a while - but, one day, people may start to behave in a different way and a new theory may be needed to predict future behaviour. This doesn't mean that the original theory was wrong or that it wasn't useful at all - only that it may not be accurate for all time.

For example, you might have a theory that house prices follow a 'bubble' pattern of several years of rapidly rising prices, followed by a sudden drop (the bubble bursts!) and then the whole cycle starts again.

The reason this pattern may occur is that, when house prices rise, people often imagine that prices will continue to rise. They may believe that there is easy money to be made by buying houses and then selling them for a profit later on. The chance of easy money sees lots of people clambering to buy houses and this does indeed cause prices to rise further.

Then, having paid a lot for their houses, some people start to struggle to make their mortgage payments. People start to realise that house prices have become ridiculously high and that people can't really afford such high prices. A degree of panic sets in - and house prices suddenly collapse as people scramble to sell property before prices fall even further.

This theory about how house prices behave may appear to be correct - for some time - but, if people start to recognise this pattern, they'll start to realise that rapidly rising house prices are often a precursor to a collapse. This knowledge makes them more cautious about buying property in the first place. They're no longer willing to pay so much for a house. As a result of such forward-thinking, the house prices bubble may never occur in the first place.

So, people change. They adjust their beliefs and their behaviour and economic theories have to adjust in turn. This doesn't mean, however, that the economists who came up with these theories were incompetent or that Economics is not a valid, scientific discipline. Economics is a science. We study patterns, but these are not the immutable patterns of physics - they are patterns of human behaviour and subject to change as humans change and adapt to the changing world they live in.

By recognising and remembering that Economics is a branch of psychology, we can avoid getting stuck with economic theories that, whilst they may have proved very useful in the past, no longer fit the way people are behaving *now* or how they are likely to behave in the future.

So, Economics is, in many ways, a branch of psychology. Understanding people helps us understand our economy. What is, perhaps, even more interesting, however, is how studying our economy can help us understand more about people.

Welfare

One of the reasons Economics is not just about money, is that there are many things that affect how well-off someone is - and money is only one of them. Indeed, the relationship between how rich people are and such things as how happy, contented or fulfilled they are, is far from clear.

To look at how well-off someone is, you may indeed consider their monetary income and their wealth, but you would also want to consider such things as their health and the access they have to high-quality healthcare. You'd look at how well-educated they are. You'd look at how pleasant and psychologically rewarding their job is. You'd look at whether they have family and friends to support them. You'd look at how much leisure time they have. You'd look at whether they have interests and hobbies. You'd look at the environment they live in and the sort of climate they enjoy - or have to put up with!

It is clearly very possible for someone who has very little money to still be very well off indeed. Even if they have little material wealth, they can still be very well provided for. They might eat healthily. They might live near to fantastic countryside or other free leisure facilities. They might have lots of friends - or, more likely, just a few very good ones. They may not own many books, but they can borrow as many books from the library - or from friends and family - as they will ever need or want.

And it is equally possible for someone who has lots of money to be very badly off. They might be very unhealthy, very lonely, very isolated, poorly educated, bored, selfish, unkind and unloved.

If we're talking about a person's general wellbeing - beyond just how much money they have - we may refer to their 'welfare.'

It is true that there probably aren't any entirely satisfactory ways of measuring a person's welfare. It can be difficult to define exactly what a person's or a country's 'welfare' refers to exactly. The point is, however, that a person's general welfare is about far, far more than how much money they have, how much income they receive or how much material wealth they command.

On many occasions, for example, surveys have attempted to find out how happy and contented people around the world are. Again, happiness is not an easy thing to measure scientifically and we often have to rely a lot on people's self-perceptions. Nevertheless, the results of these surveys often seem to suggest that some of the world's poorest people are actually amongst the world's happiest and most contented people.

A proper economist is far more concerned with people's welfare than he is with their incomes. Monetary income is only a fraction of what is important when considering a person's welfare. Similarly, a community or society can be 'rich' in many ways that don't have much to do with the movements of small green/blue/pink pieces of paper.

When referring to a person's welfare, economists often refer to the concept of 'utility.' A person's 'utility' is a measure of how well-off they are - although it isn't really anything you can actually measure as such using any sort of widely-recognised units. We might say, however, that one situation would provide a person with greater utility than would another situation. We might say that a particular decision would lead to an improvement in a person's utility.

There have been many arguments amongst economists over how useful or otherwise the concept of utility is. Perhaps its most important function, however, lies simply in reminding us (again) that a person's welfare does not have a straightforward and linear relationship with their income or wealth.

Consider this: If you are a person on a fairly low to average wage, then it could make an amazing difference to you if you won a million pounds (or even dollars!) on the lottery. You could buy a nice house, a nice car and you need never really worry about money again.

Winning another million pounds would still be wonderful and could bring you significant additional benefits, but it wouldn't make anywhere near as spectacular a difference to your life as the first million. The luxurious sports car you already own is more than adequate to get you to the golf club each day. You could buy a more expensive car or a second sports car, just for variety, but it won't really make a great difference to your life. If you're lucky enough to win a third lot of a million pounds, that might make only a very marginal difference. A fourth million might barely make a noticeable difference at all.

The point is that your second million doesn't provide anywhere near as much benefit as your first million may have brought you. Not every pound (or dollar) is worth the same - at least, in terms of the difference it makes to your overall wellbeing.

Economists are ultimately much more interested in welfare and utility than in money. Of course, if you gave a very poor person a big load of money, then you could probably transform their lives for the better. Very often, however, the relationship between the money people have and their welfare is not nearly as straightforward as many people might lazily assume.

And happiness, contentment and fulfilment are also intimately connected to life's difficulties and challenges. There is much more satisfaction and fulfilment to be gained from meeting challenges and overcoming difficulties than can ever be gained simply by spending money.

Science and Models

In studying resource problems, economists use rational and scientific methods. Economics is a science. We collect data. We consider variables. We form and test theories.

Economics, however, is very much a real world science. A physicist or chemist can often set up a carefully designed experiment in which most variables are kept constant, allowing them to see how changing one variable affects another. Economists, however, don't often have the luxury of following such methods. For example, we can't simply halve people's incomes to see what effect this has on the demand for bread. People wouldn't appreciate it!

There is a growing field of Experimental Economics where research is indeed conducted in laboratory-type conditions, with volunteers being asked to respond to a variety of scenarios and incentives. It is difficult to be confident, however, that the reactions and decisions of volunteers in a laboratory experiment will reflect at all accurately how they would behave in the real world when significant amounts of their own money and their own futures are at stake. Whilst the laws of physics are the same in the laboratory as they are in real-life scenarios, economic behaviour can't be isolated so easily.

Economists work in a rather different, but no less scientific way than those who work in laboratory-based sciences. Economists make models of the world we live in. They may be graphical, diagrammatic models. They may be mathematical models. They may be complicated models contained in the bowels of a supercomputer - or they may just be straightforward models described in a sentence or two of plain English.

These models will all be simplified models of the real world. If they weren't simplified, then we might just as well look at the real world and the real world is too complex for us to fully understand. We don't, however, want them to be too simplified - otherwise they may fail to reflect the real world or teach us anything about how the real world works.

These models can then be used to predict behaviour. Many things are difficult to predict (and Economics has the added problem that predictions themselves affect the future), but just because economists can't predict the future with absolute accuracy, this doesn't mean we aren't being rational and scientific. It doesn't mean that those predictions aren't much, much better than pure guesswork.

Furthermore, Economics is not a body of knowledge. Just like science, Economics is a rational way of looking at and understanding the world. It is not a list of things to remember. It is not about people telling you things and you being able to regurgitate that knowledge. There are no facts to learn - just tools and methods for working out the probable answers for yourself, in individual circumstances.

Economics is a set of skills, a way of thinking and a way of understanding the world. You can apply those skills to many different situations, but you won't always get the same answers - so there are no 'answers' to learn!

As a student economist, you don't, for example, learn that people will buy more of a particular good if you lower its price. There's a very good reason why you aren't taught this; because it isn't always true! It's the sort of thing a 'Business' student might be told - but an economist is supposed to have the intelligence and the skills to be able to analyse a market for themselves - they will then be able to predict whether a fall in price of a particular product in a particular place will or will not lead to more people buying that product.

Oh - and one final myth I'd like to expose here: Economists do not need to keep their skills 'up-to-date.' Situations change and economic theories change - but the essential skills of an economist never go out of date.

Scarcity

The concept of scarcity is central to a great deal of Economics and to most of the problems and challenges that economists are asked to deal with. Scarcity simply refers to the fact that we have limited - or 'scarce' resources.

Any individual country has, for example, a limited amount of farmland and a limited amount of oil. Even when we might have very large natural stocks of something, there may be only a rather limited amount that we can make available in any one year. For example, even if a country has huge supplies of coal - enough to last for many thousands of years - they can still only extract a limited amount from the ground in any one year.

At any one time, a country also has a limited supply of workers. Most goods and products require raw materials and workers to make them - and with a limited supply of raw materials and workers, we are also limited in terms of almost all the other goods we can produce, so those goods are scarce too!

Traditionally, Economics books have sought to distinguish between 'scarce resources' that we have a limited supply of and 'free resources' that we have an unlimited supply of. They might have listed such things as water and air as 'free resources' or 'free goods.' In many places in the world, however, water is actually quite scarce. And air isn't as free as we once assumed either - especially if you're talking about clean air. Clean, smog-free air is not freely available to many of the inhabitants of some of the world's largest cities. So, almost all resources are 'scarce resources' of which we have a limited supply.

The key point about scarcity is that, since we are limited in the resources and goods we have available to us, we have to make choices about what we are going to use our scarce resources for. Some projects will get the go ahead - and have resources allocated to them - and other projects will get turned down. We have to choose - and many of the decisions we have to make are difficult ones with profound and often fatal consequences.

Think about it and you'll realise that many simple, everyday decisions, can have life-changing and deadly consequences. A simple decision to have a cup of coffee is, in effect, a decision that scarce, fertile farmland in a poor country will be used to grow coffee beans for you instead of to grow food to feed the local population or some other poor people around the world.

There are billions of important decisions that have to be made every day and Economics is largely about looking at the choices we face - as individuals, businesses, nations and as a species - and helping us decide which options are the best ones to take. It is a tool for helping us make decisions. It helps us decide how to allocate and use our scarce resources to achieve many of the things we consider are worthwhile in life.

Despite our scarce resources, we have a great many needs and wants. There are certain basic needs that we must fulfil in order simply to survive and to continue the existence of our species. We need water, food, shelter and warmth and, to continue the species, we need a lot of people to have sex occasionally. Lots of other things, we don't actually need, but we certainly want them and, even in terms of food, drink and sex, we tend to want a lot more than we actually need.

It is often said that humans have unlimited wants. In other words, no matter how much we have, we will always want more. The problem of having unlimited wants and desires, but only scarce resources with which to provide for our wants and satisfy our desires, is often referred to as 'the basic economic problem' - and this mismatch of wants and resources is often given as the main justification for the existence of Economics as a discipline of study in the first place.

However, it is important to stop and question whether we really do have unlimited wants. Does there, perhaps, come a point where having more goods and services no longer makes us any better off?

Politicians often behave as if they're assuming that producing and consuming ever more goods and services will make us better off. They often behave as if this neverending acceleration in the rate at which we produce and consume things might actually be the only way to make ourselves better off. They may think that the job of an economist is simply to tell them how we can produce and consume ever more and more and yet more goods and services.

Actually, any intelligent and responsible economist will realise that making us better off is not simply a matter of producing and consuming ever more goods and services.

In fact, it's about time we thought about whether we might actually make ourselves better off by producing and consuming far less. An obvious example is with food. Many people are obese because they've eaten too much food. It may be politically-incorrect to point this out, but it happens to be true. Many people would clearly be better off if they ate less food. The same goes for the consumption of many other goods.

Scarcity is frequently a very real and pressing problem. Often, however, it is a scarcity of intelligent thinkers, able to reassess the lazy assumptions of the societies we live in, that lies at the heart of our most embarrassing problems and shortages.

Decisions

As I've said, economists are fascinated by people's decisions. We look at the decisions people make and wonder whether they - and the societies they live in - could have been better off if they had made different decisions.

In order to learn to make better decisions, it would seem sensible to start by asking: What makes a decision a good decision? One possible answer to this question is that a decision is a good one if there were no better options available. This brings us to one of the most central and important concepts in all of Economics: Opportunity Cost.

The idea behind 'opportunity cost' is that every decision we make, every option we pick, has a very real cost. We're not talking about money here, of course - we're talking about something much more important. We're talking about lost opportunities.

Every day, we face choices. We have to decide between alternative options. And many of the most important decisions we have to make are about how we use our scarce and valuable resources.

For example, we have limited reserves of oil and we are also limited in terms of how much we can extract and refine each year. We have to decide how each barrel of oil will be used. Some projects get the oil they need, but we don't have enough oil for every project we can think of - so, somewhere along the line, some other projects are going to lose out.

When we use oil to fuel our car on the school run each morning, when we could have walked the kids to school, we've effectively taken that oil away from someone else or from some other purpose. That fuel could have been used to take vaccines to a poor community in the developing world. Thanks to our decision to use that fuel for the school run, that poor community will have to go without. An important opportunity will have been missed.

When an option is chosen, that option may bring us many benefits - but, at the same time, we are missing out on the alternative options that we turned down and we are foregoing the benefits that the best one of those options could have brought us. The concept of 'opportunity cost' is simply that we might judge an option by asking whether a better one is available.

The 'opportunity cost' of a decision is equal to the value of the benefits you miss out on as a result of choosing one option over another. If the benefits from an alternative option would have been more valuable than the benefits you'd receive from the option you actually chose, then perhaps you made a poor decision and chose the wrong option!

As a simple example, the real cost - the opportunity cost - of going to the cinema last night and watching a film was not five pounds (or however much a ticket costs now). The real cost of going to the cinema is the benefit I (and, indirectly, others) would have received if, instead of going to the cinema, I had, for example, read a book.

I'm not talking about a book that I would have read anyway. If I didn't go to the cinema. then I could have read an extra book - an additional book that I otherwise wouldn't have read. If I could have read such a book that would have been far more entertaining and far more educational than the film I watched at the cinema, then going to the cinema doesn't seem like a very good decision. I could have spent my time more wisely.

Our societies generally obsess about financial costs - looking at how much things cost us in terms of the money we spend. But, compared to opportunity cost, financial costs are insubstantial and almost meaningless. For example, we might say that the financial cost of providing a hospital bed is five hundreds pounds a day. But what does this really mean? What does it mean in human terms? Not much really!

Now let's think of that hospital bed in terms of opportunity cost. A hospital can only treat a limited number of people on any one time. It has, as we describe it, a limited number of 'beds.' Not everyone gets the operation or treatment they desire, so a decision to treat one patient is, effectively, a decision to deny treatment to someone else. The true cost - the opportunity cost - of providing a patient with a hospital bed for a day is that some other person has to go without a day's treatment. Some such people will die as a result of not having had that treatment. Others will merely suffer additional pain and discomfort. This seems especially tough if the person who got treatment only needed treatment because they smoked too much, drank too much or ate too much! Opportunity costs can be very, very real and painful costs.

Power

Any society has to have ways of making important decisions about scarce resources. Who will these scarce resources be allocated to? What will they be used to create or provide? What shall be produced and who shall it be produced for? Each society must decide who gets to make these important economic decisions.

There is, of course, more than one fundamental way to run an economy and, over the centuries, different societies have used different systems for making the important decisions about how scarce resources are allocated.

In some societies, a lot of economic power rests in the hands of individuals. People are allowed a lot of freedom to decide how they will try to make a living and what they will do with their lives. In this sort of society, a lot of decisions are decided by 'market forces' - in other words, decisions come about as a result of individuals freely interacting and bargaining with each other.

In some societies, large businesses have a lot of economic power. In some societies, religious organisations make a lot of key economic decisions. And, in many societies, the government and the state have enormous economic power. They might control a large part of the economy directly and may impose strict rules and regulations about how individuals and businesses can behave. In each society, the boundaries between the various spheres of control and spheres of influence will be drawn in different places.

This balance of power between individuals, businesses and the state is a very important concern of Economics. It is fundamental to a lot of economic matters and has a huge impact on people's general welfare and wellbeing.

Clearly, some people or organisations may be better at making decisions than others. Some people have a better understanding of the way certain things work and are better at predicting the ramifications of their decisions. So, it may make sense to put the economic decision making power in the hands of people who are good at it. Putting decisions in the hands of educated, skilled and competent decision-makers might produce decisions that are more likely to benefit society in general.

Unfortunately, there is often a tendency for people or organisations to allocate resources according to their own selfish interests, instead of according to what is good for others or for society in general. When a government, for example, allocates resources, are they acting for the good of the nation or are they allocating resources in such a way as to try to get themselves re-elected? Are they looking after themselves and their own supporters at the expense of everyone else? Are government ministers trying to help the nation or are they just looking after their own careers?

It may seem OK to have a village chief making economic decisions on behalf of the entire tribe, if he happens to be very good at it and doesn't behave in a selfish way. Unfortunately, it's usually the incompetent, selfish leaders who are best at lying and cheating their way into positions of power in the first place.

But there's something else that's very important here - something perhaps even more fundamental; something to do with freedom. The thing is that your welfare is greatly affected by how much freedom you have. To be human, to feel alive, it's important that you have some sort of freedom to make decisions about your own life. If all the decisions about your life are made by other people, they may be extremely good at making decisions and they may make lots of decisions that make you better off, but something would be missing; your fundamental freedom to make decisions for yourself, even if those decisions aren't always very good ones.

Our welfare as human beings, depends not just on such things as what material goods and services we have available to us - and such things do depend on good decisions as to how we use our scarce resources - but also on such things as how much freedom we have. Without freedom, we're all a lot poorer. We can be immensely rich in terms of material goods, but still be desperately poor.

Specialisation and Trade

The concept of specialisation is essentially a very simple one.

Imagine a primitive society where each individual is self-sufficient and provides for their own individual needs entirely by themselves. They each go hunting by themselves, they fish in the river, they collect nuts and berries from the woods, they each start their own fires and they do their own individual cooking. They build and maintain their own shelters and make their own clothes.

This might not sound like a bad lifestyle, but it isn't a very efficient one. Each individual will be good at some tasks, but not very good at others and each individual will be wasting a lot of time moving from one task to another.

Imagine, instead, that we organise this society so that each person concentrates on one or two tasks that they happen to be particularly good at. They get the other things they need by trading with other people in the village.

Some people, for example, might become full-time fishermen. They concentrate on this particular task and become rather good at it. They develop special tools to help them work more efficiently. At the end of each day's fishing, they have far more fish than they need for themselves, so they trade their surplus of fish for other things. Some people become specialist hunters, some gather nuts and berries - and so on.

The effects of such a reorganisation can be much more dramatic than you might imagine. Rather than producing just a minor improvement in food production, the villagers might well find that their lives are radically transformed. Instead of barely managing to survive, they might soon find themselves producing a considerable surplus. Instead of having to spend all their time providing essentials, they can now spend time on leisure pursuits, games and entertainment. They can spend time exploring and experimenting. They can provide themselves with luxury items or trade their surpluses for goods from other villages.

Further specialisation might see people becoming carpenters or blacksmiths who can provide tools for other people to work even more efficiently. In time, there may be dozens or, in a larger community, even hundreds of specialised occupations and a complex trading system to enable everyone to trade their surpluses for the other things they need or want.

When the production of even a single product is split into separate tasks and these tasks are split between different people, this type of specialisation is known as 'the division of labour' and often produces spectacular further increases in production. With this division of labour, not only are people specialising in the production of one particular product, they are often specialising in just one of the many specific tasks that are required in that production process.

Ask people how we developed our rich, modern societies and they might well point to the benefits of technology. In many ways, however, it is actually the benefits of specialisation that are more fundamentally important in improving our living standards.

Even the benefits of advanced technology are only possible thanks to specialisation. From blacksmiths to nuclear scientists, people have developed their technological knowledge, skills and expertise by being able to specialise in their particular area of study. They've been able to do this only because other people have specialised in such things as producing food and building houses. How far would we have got at developing our technology if everyone had to produce all their own food for themselves?

Fast forward to today, however, and it's important to ask ourselves whether specialisation has gone too far. We can all see how having someone specialise as a blacksmith or as a doctor can have enormous benefits for society. Some jobs today, however, are so ludicrously specialised, we might wonder whether they have any real purpose at all. Does a 'Diversity Enhancement Manager' really provide a useful function for society?

And we also have to remember that greater specialisation requires a more complex trading arrangement - and that there are significant costs and problems that can be caused by having a complicated trading system. Financial crises, for example, are often essentially caused by a breakdown in trading procedures. Some people fail to pay what they owe for goods they've been supplied. Consequently, other people can't pay what they owe and so on until we have a widespread crisis on our hands. Greater specialisation requires a more complicated trading arrangement - and the more complex it is, the more likely it is to break down and the bigger the problems when it does break down.

And then there's the whole question of the negative effects that specialisation can have on workers. It's easy to see why someone might rather enjoy specialising as a musician or as an aircraft designer, but many jobs are specialised in a way that doesn't make working life fun at all. We can see how a great sense of fulfilment can be achieved by specialising as a car designer or even as an ordinary mechanic, but what about someone who just put tyres on wheels - and that's all they ever do whilst at work?

When people specialise in a task such as fitting a particular piece of plastic to a particular model of car all day long or spend all day assembling the same damn model of smartphone for long hours, day after day, you can see how repetition and boredom can - in some cases, quite literally - sap people's will to live. At the time of writing, for example, there is considerable concern over the suicide rates in some Chinese factories where people mass produce well-known technology products.

Effectively, many people in the modern world are forced to specialise to such a degree that it takes all the interest and variety out of their work. Can that really be good for those individuals or even for society in general? It may appear to be an efficient and productive way of working, but is it? Might the repetition and boredom in fact be a price that isn't worth paying? Might such specialisation actually result in far more problems than it is worth?

The Market

A lot of economic decisions are made 'by markets' and are determined by 'market forces.'

If you study Economics for any sort of formal qualification, you'll probably spend a lot of time studying how markets work. You'll hear about 'the price mechanism' and 'the invisible hand' of the market. You might spend a little bit of time learning definitions of what a market is - sometimes rather vague definitions, such as 'the market is where demand meets supply.' You'll also be spending many hours looking at, drawing, manipulating and analysing countless demand and supply diagrams.

Even with all this studying, however, your actual understanding of markets may still be very limited. The trouble is that, useful as demand and supply diagrams often are, they can also lead students to skip over and fail to understand the much more fundamental basics of how a market actually works and the very important functions it performs on our behalf. Perhaps, however, you'll find the following example rather revealing:

When Russia was part of the Soviet Union and had a communist government, they had a command economy where the state dictated to people where they would work, what they would produce, how much they had to produce and who would get to have the products they made.

By the late 1980s, this economic system was collapsing alongside the communist political system and the Soviet Union itself. New leaders were emerging and some of these believed that Russia should move to a more western-style, 'market-led' economy. One of these people was

Boris Yeltsin, who, in 1991, became the first president of the new Russian Federation.

One of the problems, however, was that it was highly questionable whether Boris actually understood how market economies work. His questionable understanding of markets was laid bare when he arrived at a baker's shop, journalists in tow, on one of his walkabouts around Moscow. At the time, there was a severe shortage of bread in Moscow and this baker was taking advantage of this shortage and was charging very high prices for his bread and making a lot of profit in the process. He was 'profiteering.'

Boris Yeltsin went practically berserk, shouting at and severely castigating the baker for making extra money by taking advantage of the shortage. Yet, when you think about it, his anger made no sense at all - unless you believe it was merely a political stunt to make himself more popular. In many ways, the baker was actually doing the people of Moscow an enormous favour. He was doing exactly what needed to be done if a market economy is to work properly.

There was a shortage of bread because not enough of it was being produced. This problem will only be solved when people invest in new baking facilities - but people will only invest in these new facilities if they can see their way to making a decent profit from doing so.

In a free market, prices play an incredibly important signalling role that Boris did not appear to understand. When there's a shortage of bread, consumers are desperate to get their hands on bread and are prepared to pay extra in order to do so. Suppliers realise they can increase the prices they charge to their customers and yet still manage to sell all the bread they have available.

By charging very high prices for his bread, the baker in our example was signalling to potential investors that there was money to be made from making bread. High prices encourage investment in new baking facilities by showing that such investments can be highly profitable. Investments are made, new supplies come on line and the shortage problems are solved.

Any interference that stopped the baker from charging high prices, could discourage other people and businesses from investing in new baking facilities. Rather than helping consumers, such interference might well lead to continued shortages for a long time to come. No-one's likely to invest in a bakery if the price of bread is artificially low.

In a market system, in which prices are free to change, a remarkable thing happens! Buyers try to get themselves a good deal. They only pay what they have to pay - and this helps prevent wasteful surpluses of things people don't want.

Similarly, sellers are free to charge buyers as much as they can get away with - in other words, as much as buyers are willing to pay. And it is sellers trying to charge as much as they can get away with that actually helps to prevent shortages. High prices are the signal to increase production in preparation for the future.

It may not seem fair that the Moscow baker in our example exploited the situation he found himself in to make extra profits. It may not seem fair that he charged high prices when he could have afforded to charge less. But I tell you what is even more unfair: people starving to death because there is not enough food to go around! The people of Moscow demanded bread. The baker had the

42

forethought to produce bread. He was doing what the people wanted - meeting their essential needs - so the market and the price mechanism rewarded him for this.

Market forces help to prevent shortages. The price system helps allocate resources to where they are needed. Prices are not about fairness - they're about avoiding people starving to death!

Profit

Profits play an important role in a market economy. If is often said that businesses exist in order to make a profit. They sell things for money and some of that money is used to cover their costs - buy materials, pay workers, pay rent etc. What they have left is their profits - which, in one way or another, get distributed to the people who own the business.

Profit is supposed to be a reward for when businesses do a good job of providing consumers with what they want (although, unfortunately, profits are often made through less sanitary methods!). For ordinary workers, their wages might be thought of as their profits from the work that they do.

The thirst for profits and the ongoing quest for ever-higher profits (or earnings) are often presented as being the key driving forces behind our economies - but real life isn't that simple! In real life, people run businesses for many different reasons - it isn't all about making a profit. People go to work for many different reasons - it isn't all about earning money to pay for things they want.

People's motivations are many and varied. A lot of work-related and business-related activity, for example, is actually something to do with people's psychological or social needs. They want to feel useful, they want to feel valued and they may want to meet and make friends with other people.

Profit-seeking is an important motivation in market economies, but it is only one of many motivations - and a good economist should take care to remember this.

Government

Economists tend to spend a lot of time studying how markets work. It is important to remember, however, that, in most modern societies, markets are not the only way in which resources are allocated. Our world, today, is dominated by the decisions of powerful nation-states. A lot of economic decisions are made, not by the market as such, but by the state. Even the decisions made by the market are often severely constrained and heavily influenced by the state. Markets usually operate firmly in the shadow of the state.

Economists do not confine themselves, therefore, to understanding how markets operate. We also study how governments operate as they allocate and use a sizeable proportion of the resources available to our societies and are hugely influential in how businesses and individuals allocate and use the rest of our available resources. It would be silly to ignore how governments work and how good a job - or otherwise - they do in allocating our precious resources.

Imagine a very primitive society, with no formal leadership and no laws or commonly-accepted rules of behaviour. People do their own thing. They make their own decisions about the scarce resources they have control of. With everyone doing their own thing, however, there is always the potential for disputes and conflict. In a very primitive society, if there is a serious dispute of any kind, then matters might well be settled by force or the threat of force. The people who can bring the most force to bear tend to win the argument over how things are done - and they're the ones who get to decide how resources are used.

At some point, societies tend to develop some form of government that can make judgements when disputes arise (and thus, perhaps, avoid violence). It can also help organise people in order that they can work together and achieve things through collaboration that they might not be able to achieve individually. People might work together to hunt, to fish or to protect themselves from other tribes or natural dangers.

In its simplest form, this 'government' may be a leader who tells everyone else what to do. This leader might become leader simply because they have the fighting skills to force other people to obey them. On the other hand, someone might become leader because other people respect their ability to make wise decisions on behalf of the community. In some societies, someone manages to become leader because others have become convinced that God or 'a god' has chosen them to become leader.

Some communities might have a group of elders who make decisions. Some communities might even develop a form of democracy where most members of the community share in some forms of collective decision-making.

Whatever form the government takes, the existence of a 'government' generally means that there is now an additional way in which resource decisions are made. Economic decisions are no longer made only by individuals or by groups of individuals freely choosing to act together. The leadership or 'government' now has the power to override some of the decisions taken by individuals.

In almost all modern societies, the power of the

government ultimately comes from its ability to use force to override individual decisions. Some people might have chosen to follow their leaders, even if no force had been threatened. However, choice doesn't usually come into it anymore, because nearly all of us - even those of us who live in what we regard as the 'free world' - live in a society where we live under the constant threat of government action and government force if we don't follow government instructions. We may have the option of leaving the country where we live, but, even then, we'd usually have to move to another country and be forcibly subjected to the rules and regulations of that country's government. Some countries of the past have gone as far as to operate a 'command economy' where the state dictates what will be produced, dictates what prices will be charged and even dictates to people what jobs they must do. You might just be told that you will be working as a cleaner in a certain factory - and that would be it. You would have no choice in the matter - unless, that is, you fancied being worked to death in some labour camp in Siberia!

As individuals, we are clearly capable of making some very bad decisions. But, if we allow the state to make some decisions on our behalf, how confident can we be that the state will make better decisions than if those decisions had been left to individuals?

It does seem very plausible that it is possible to make ourselves better off as a society by allowing the state to make some decisions on our behalf. Furthermore, sometimes, collective decisions may be better than individual ones, regardless of which way a decisions actually goes.

It doesn't seem a great detraction from our

freedoms if we allow the state to raise a little money through taxes so that it can intervene to stop people starving in the streets or to provide everyone with basic education, so that everyone can at least read and write.

And, to some extent, the state can essentially provide us with freedoms. How much freedom would we have if the state didn't protect us from murderers and thieves? How much 'freedom' to pick a job would we have if we couldn't even read? Could we really argue that we would be better off or even just 'more free' without basic law-enforcement agencies or without basic educational facilities?

Generally, people accept that by having some sort of state, some sort of basic laws and regulations and by having some level of taxation to pay for basic services, we can all be better off. Markets are very far from perfect - and the state can sometimes improve the situation compared to what we'd have if we just left everyone to do their own thing.

However, if we allow the state to control everything, we'll be very badly off, because, without the freedom to make our own decisions on anything, we're pretty sure that would be awful. Even if we were rich, that wouldn't make up for having no freedom at all. We'd be downright miserable!

Extreme 'command economies' don't tend to make people particularly rich anyway, as they tend to be beset by their own particular economic difficulties.

One of their biggest problems is that they often struggle to match demand and supply and so tend to be beset by problems with surpluses and shortages. The government of a command

48

economy has to make decisions on how much of each product to produce (and what prices to charge and so on) and they often get things wrong, often resulting in severe shortages.

With a market system, shortages and surpluses affect the prices of goods and result in a sort of self-correcting economy. Shortages lead to higher prices - thus encouraging people to produce more. Surpluses lead to falling prices, thus encouraging businesses to cut back on production and perhaps make something else instead. This is the price mechanism in action, signalling what needs to be produced.

In a command economy, people aren't free to change what they produce. They aren't free to change the prices they charge. They aren't free to choose what jobs they do or what businesses they start. Furthermore, the government, responsible as it is for so many production decisions, is often a bit slow to react. Consequently, shortages and surpluses can persist for a long time, which is rather wasteful and very annoying if you have to queue for hours to get something you need. The dying days of the Soviet Union - perhaps history's most famous command economy - was characterised by massive queues at the shops.

Shortages in official shops are also exacerbated because some of the goods that were supposed to reach official, state-controlled shops and suppliers, find their way, instead, on to the 'black market.' People realise they can make extra money by selling shortage goods privately, outside of official channels, for much more than the official state-controlled prices. This leads to even greater shortages in official shops, longer queues and, therefore, even more of an incentive for people to trade goods on the black market.

Another problem is that command economies often struggle to deal with the problems of discontent that stem from people's lack of freedom. When people don't want to do what they are told, live where they are told to live and work where they are told to work, the government often resorts to force and oppression to get the population to obey it's commands. They often end up developing an oppressive - and resource-hungry - policing and internal security system in order to enforce the state's decisions, enforce the restrictions the state places on individual freedoms and to repress the many people who demand more freedom and what they regard as basic human rights.

In the UK or the US and in many other countries, we tend to think of ourselves as having a lot of freedom. Relative to how things are done in some other countries, this is true, but, when you think about it, the state still imposes huge restrictions on us.

There are many goods and services that you can't be employed in providing, because the state has made it illegal to provide those goods and services. In many places in the US, for example, you can't get a job in the gambling industry, because many forms of gambling are illegal there. How ironic that 'the land of the free' has such draconian restrictions on how people spend their own money!

Even when a certain business activity is legal, there may be so many licence requirements, regulations, restrictions and such heavy taxes that making a profit is virtually impossible. In effect, the state has made the decision that you can't do it, even though it is technically legal.

There's little doubt that both free-market

capitalism and state-control have their problems. So, at what point do the disadvantages of state intervention and control start to outweigh the benefits? In which areas of our lives should we allow state control - and which areas of our lives should the state stay the hell out of?

To some extent, these are questions for philosophy and politics to answer, but it is also an Economics question. We have limited, scarce resources. We want to make the best possible use of them. So, when is it best to allow resources decisions to be taken by individuals negotiating with each other in a free market and when is it best to allow the state to make resource decisions on our behalf? These are questions that economists and politicians have grappled with for centuries. We may never all agree on the answers, but these issues remain fundamental to our welfare and to our future success as individuals and as a society.

Firms

An interesting way to think of a firm - such as a partnership, company, corporation or any other business - is as a sort of mini command economy.

The employees of the firm - whether they are ordinary workers or managers of some kind - essentially have to do as they are told. Each worker generally has a line manager - a boss - who tells them what to do.

It's true that there are limits on the power their boss has. Their boss can only really order them to do things that are legal and the worker's contract may further restrict what activities they can be ordered to undertake. And, ultimately (at least in most countries), a worker who doesn't like their job can simply leave it - if they can afford to do so - and try to find another one elsewhere.

Nevertheless, whilst a worker is working for a firm, it is, in many ways, like working in a sort of mini-dictatorship (It often feels like that too!). It's just that, instead of a Prime Minister or President, there's a business owner or a Chief Executive Officer. Instead of a Parliament or Congress, there may be a Board of Directors. So, in a sense, firms are like mini-fiefdoms - islands of central control.

If there were no firms at all, then individuals would have to negotiate with each other over every little thing they needed to cooperate over in order to achieve anything. Everyone would be a 'freelance' - hiring themselves out for individual tasks. For some professions, this might work very well. For example, journalists and illustrators often work on a freelance basis. In other professions and industries, however, the constant need for negotiation over every individual task would probably make a freelance system unworkable. Imagine having to negotiate to hire a secretary every time you wanted a letter typed - and never being sure of which secretary would be available at any particular time. Imagine having to negotiate for chefs, waiters and cleaners every day in order to run a restaurant - ever day having to negotiate afresh how much people will be paid. Thus, in order to cut down on the time and energy needed to negotiate, firms employ workers on a much longer term basis - and thus form these mini-fiefdoms.

In a sense, therefore, firms represent a sort of compromise between a completely open market economy populated only by individuals and an economy completely controlled by an all-powerful government. As such, they can benefit, in the same way as governments, from the ability to coordinate individuals and resources without getting bogged down in constant negotiations.

On the other hand, they can suffer from the same problems as governments. By having the ability to dictate things without negotiation, they can lose track of demand and supply and end up with problems of shortages or surpluses (such as having huge stocks of goods they are unable to sell). They can become bogged down in bureaucracy. They may also become self-serving; losing sight of the individual owners, customers and workers they are supposed to be benefiting.

In a sense, the difference between a command economy and a capitalist economy is merely that a capitalist economy is made up of many miniature command economies - with each mini command economy being known as a company, a business, a charity, an organisation or a family.

Firms, in a way, are free market organisations, because the individuals that make up the firm are voluntarily coordinating their actions, supposedly for the common good. This sounds good in theory. In practice, however, the experience of working for a firm - especially a large one - can often be much more like slaving under the direction of a powerful dictator.

The existence of firms brings many advantages, but, especially when they get very big, they can also bring many problems that aren't too far away from the problems caused by an over-powerful state.

Intervention

One of the reasons governments feel justified in interfering in markets is because people often feel that markets sometimes 'fail' in some way and that something ought to be done to correct this failure.

Sometimes, businesses behave in what we might consider to be deeply unethical ways. Sometimes they treat their workers badly. Sometimes, they show no regard for the environment.

One of the most common problems is when businesses try to get rid of competition. Imagine you have a village or small town with two grocery shops. Neither shop can charge unreasonably high prices, because, if they did, everyone would simply go and shop in the other store. Competition keeps prices low. You can see, then, why the owner of one shop might be tempted to buy the other one. He can then charge much higher prices in both shops without having to worry so much about the competition. Alternatively, the owners of the two shops might get together (traditionally, this is done in a smoke-filled room!) and agree on a secret deal that they will both charge high prices. Either idea might be regarded as 'anti-competitive' and unfair.

Sometimes, it is not individual businesses, but the market as a whole that seems to be acting unfairly. Imagine, for example, that the state did not supply any schools and left education services entirely up to individuals and businesses in the free market. The result would probably be that the children of rich, well-educated parents received a good education, but children with poor or under-educated parents did not. This, again, seems very unfair.

It often seems reasonable, therefore, for the

state/government to interfere in the market in some way. Sometimes they provide services themselves - such as when they provide schools. Sometimes, they regulate and control what private businesses can do and how they can behave.

The trouble is that there is never any end to the demands that the government should 'do something' about something - that they should stop individuals, companies or markets doing things we might consider to be unreasonable or unfair.

The government is bombarded by continual demands that it should interfere and regulate in order to 'enforce standards,' to 'control excesses,' to 'prevent abuses' and to 'protect consumers.' Further demands are made that the government should intervene to keep interest rates low, boost jobs, protect jobs, reduce unemployment, modernise our infrastructure, control inflation, boost growth, boost demand for various goods and services, encourage exports, encourage the take-up of new technology and all manner of other things!

Individually, such demands might sound reasonable, but if we don't draw the line somewhere and put a limit on what the state is allowed to interfere with, then we end up with a command economy where every economic decision is dictated by the state - and then we'll have precious few freedoms left!

Another problem is that every time the government interferes in the market, whilst this interference might appear to help in some ways, it almost always has unintended and unwanted effects in other ways - often far beyond the specific market the intervention is aimed at. For a start, state interventions in the market need to be paid for. That often means higher taxes and increased costs to businesses - and these things have huge repercussions across the whole economy. Almost any state intervention in the markets is going to have knock-on effects - many of them unintended and many of them largely unforeseen!

Sometimes, state intervention completely fails to have the effect it was intended to have, anyway. Sometimes it even produces the opposite result to what was intended and wanted.

For example, suppose the government wants to encourage people to buy electric cars. They offer a grant to anyone who buys one. You might imagine this would encourage people to buy electric cars - but it might not! For a start, once you announce this new scheme, most people will refuse to buy an electric car until the scheme actually begins. Until the grants become available, they'll be fewer electric cars bought than normally. Then, once the scheme is running, the manufacturers may take advantage of the scheme by increasing their prices - so that the extra money effectively goes to them rather than to the customer.

In due course, the money for the scheme will run out - but, now that people are used to having a subsidy to buy electric cars, they may refuse to buy an electric car without one. They may now anticipate that there might be a new scheme in the future - and may refuse to buy an electric car until there is one. All in all, you might end up with far fewer electric cars sold than if the government had not intervened at all!

And when the state intervenes in the education system, can we really expect that a bureaucrat somewhere deep in a government office complex really knows or even cares what is best for your child? Is a bureaucratic, command-driven, state-controlled system able to recognise and employ the best teachers? The state intervenes to 'ensure' every child gets a good education - but do they achieve this aim? Clearly not!

Ultimately, it is, in any case, very difficult to assess the impact of state intervention in the markets. When we look at the results of government intervention, we don't really know what to compare them with, because we don't know what the result of allowing a free market would be. State intervention affects practically every corner of the economy - so we don't really have any markets left that are even remotely free of the knock-on effects of government intervention.

It is, therefore, very difficult to know whether the problems we witness in any market are genuine market failures or whether they are actually the unintended knock-on consequences of government intervention. For example, when businesses seem to be charging unfairly high prices, is this really a market failure as such, or is it the result of lack of competition caused by government taxes and regulations discouraging potential competitors from setting up in business? The government may propose state intervention to bring down high prices, but, without government intervention, prices might never have got so high in the first place.

All of these many problems and difficulties - along with many others - contribute to making it very difficult to decide how much the state should interfere in the workings of the economy. When there's a problem, is it the market that is at fault? When is state intervention the answer to market failure - and when is it the cause of the problem in the first place?

It's no wonder that arguments over the extent of state intervention are at the centre of a large proportion of debates and arguments over how an economy should be run. How much of the economy should be in the public sector, controlled directly by the government? How tightly should private individuals and firms be regulated and controlled?

Efficiency

It is a common saying that 'you can't get something for nothing.' In a sense, however, you sometimes can, because most processes - including the production processes used in making nearly every manufactured good we own - involve a considerable amount of waste. If we wasted fewer materials or made more effective use of people's time, then we'd be producing things more 'efficiently' and we could, effectively, get something for nothing.

There are, of course, many different ways of improving the efficiency of a particular factory or a particular production process. Changing the layout of a factory, using improved technology and providing better training for workers are just a few possible examples.

The concept of efficiency is at the heart of a lot of Economics. Economists like to show how, by organising ourselves more effectively, we can reduce waste and get more out for less put in.

This type of efficiency - in simple terms; getting more out for less put in - is the sort most people will be familiar with and is known as 'technical efficiency' or 'productive efficiency.' This is the type of efficiency that is often referred to by employers, whether they are manufacturers, service providers or government departments. Again, when efficiency is mentioned in news reports, this is the sort of efficiency they are probably referring to. (Although, often, when firms talk about 'improvements in efficiency,' they're not really talking about efficiency at all - they just want their workers to work harder for less money!)

There is, however, another type of efficiency which

is often ignored, but which is incredibly important. This other type of efficiency is known as 'allocative efficiency.' Allocative efficiency is concerned with whether our scarce resources are being allocated to their best possible uses. Are resources being allocated to where they will do the most good? Whilst a lot of attention is paid to productive efficiency, it is allocative efficiency which is, in many ways, far more important.

A simple example will demonstrate the difference between productive efficiency and allocative efficiency. Productive efficiency is: How can we best set up factories to make smartphones? Allocative efficiency is: Should we be allocating our scarce and valuable resources to making smartphones in the first place? Is there actually a better use for our resources than making smartphones?

Our global economy expends vast resources on designing, manufacturing, distributing and using modern smartphones. It's all very well asking whether these phones could be made slightly more efficiently, but this shouldn't stop us seriously considering the question of whether we should be designing, manufacturing, distributing and using them at all. Are smartphones really being mainly used for productive purposes - or are they mainly just being used as a means of wasting time and distracting people from the things they know they really ought to be getting on with?

If productive efficiency is concerned with how we achieve certain things, allocative efficiency is concerned with the much bigger question of what we are achieving and what we ought to be trying to achieve - as individuals, as a society and as a species.

As a species, we have huge productive capabilities. We can produce huge quantities of goods and services. We are, however, using vast resources in order to make those products and wasting much of those resources along the way - that's productive inefficiency. Even more worryingly, however, we are largely producing things which do us little or no good whatsoever or even harm us - that's allocative inefficiency. We can be producing certain goods in huge numbers - but if those goods do us little or no good and provide few, if any, benefits, then perhaps we should be allocating our valuable resources to something else!

Scale

Over the past couple of centuries in particular, mankind has been conducting a huge and ambitious, but also very risky and dangerous experiment - a grand experiment to see what can be gained if you do things on a huge scale.

What if, instead of each family having a small farm on which they can provide enough food for themselves and a small surplus, we have enormous farms capable of feeding thousands of people? What if, instead of people spinning cloth and making clothes in their own backrooms, we have huge factories producing cotton products on a vast scale?

Towns, then larger towns, then cities were built to supply the workers needed in our huge factory complexes and their associated supply industries. We built huge factories, then chains of factories, then massive production ecosystems spanning the globe, involving hundreds of thousands of people cooperating to make and distribute a particular product.

The result of this experiment has been huge increases in our productive capabilities - but alongside such advantages, our strategy has brought considerable disadvantages and even bigger risks!

The advantages gained from working on a large scale, are often referred to as The Economies of Scale. Cars, for example, may be able to be produced more cheaply and more efficiently in a large factory using an assembly line with thousands of workers or robots than they can be produced by a few people working in a small garage. Furthermore, a large multinational company with dozens of factories and hundreds of specialist suppliers may be able to produce cars particularly efficiently.

However, it is important to understand that there is no general rule that says that big is better. Some products can be most effectively produced on a small scale. Most of the best novels, the best paintings, the best pieces of music were each produced by a single artist.

And the disadvantages of working on a huge scale can be very considerable.

When an entire product is made from scratch in a single place using locally-produced materials and finally sold to a local customer, there is very little need for transport of raw materials, part-finished goods or finished goods.

Many modern goods, however, are produced using a large-scale operation that is heavily dependent on transport. Raw materials may need to be transported thousands of miles to hundreds of parts-producing factories around the world. These parts then need to be transported to a final assembly line. The finished products are often then transported to counties all around the world. Due to transport costs, this can often seem to be a deeply inefficient and wasteful system - and, in many ways, it is.

One of the problems is that many modern manufacturing systems were developed in times when fuel was extremely cheap. Cheap oil from the Middle-East made transport ridiculously cheap. Furthermore, few people were worried about the environmental impact of burning fossil fuels. Not many people were aware of the greenhouse effect and even fewer cared.

With fuel costs many, many times greater than

they were a few decades ago and increasing concerns about the dire environmental consequences of burning fossil fuels, our globalised manufacturing systems don't seem such a good idea as they once did.

Incentives

If you want to make a business, a charity, a public body or an entire country more successful, this generally involves getting people - be they workers or customers or suppliers or families - to change their behaviour in some way. If you run a business, you want workers to work more efficiently. If you run a country, you might want people to live healthier lifestyles or to buy more locally-produced goods.

If you want people to change the decisions they make, it helps to understand how they make decisions and the things that influence their decisions. As I said, Economics is a branch of psychology!

Of course, there are many things - biology, genes, upbringing etc. - that can affect the decisions that people make. In many situations, however, it's not really possible to do anything about these things. We can't usually change a person's genes or go back and change history to change the way a person was brought up.

One of the key things an economist does, therefore, in order to understand how to change people's behaviour, is to look at the more immediate incentives people face when they make their decisions. If we want to make a better society and a better world, then we may wish to influence people and help them make better decisions. This is where incentives come in. Through understanding the incentives people face, we can see how we might be able to alter those incentives in order to persuade people to act differently - in ways we might consider to be more beneficial for the people themselves, for their employers, for our society in general and for the planet we live on.

There are, essentially, two kinds of incentives. Sometimes we use the carrot. Sometimes we use the stick. As a simple example, we may want people to do more to look after the environment. We may use the carrot - finding ways to reward those who act responsibly towards the environment. Farmers, for example, are sometimes paid subsidies to reward them for leaving hedgerows in place and thus providing a habitat for wildlife. And we may use the stick - punishing decisions which damage the environment - such as making people with gas-guzzling cars pay extra tax. This might discourage people from buying inefficient cars in the future.

This idea of using incentives might seem all fairly straightforward, but it's amazing how often problems arise because people have failed to consider the incentives that are in operation.

As an example, most employees are paid an hourly wage - a set amount of money for each hour that they work. Is it any wonder then, that many of these people don't make very good use of their time at work? If they work hard throughout an eight hour day, work efficiently and do a really good job, they still get paid exactly the same amount as if they had been really lazy during those eight hours and done the absolute minimum they thought they could get away with.

An hourly wage system may encourage workers to work long hours - because the more hours they work, the more they get paid - but it doesn't, in itself, encourage them to work hard or diligently or efficiently.

An hourly wage can even encourage workers to be lazy, because, if they are lazy and work inefficiently, you may have to pay them overtime in order to get essential work finished. In a way, they are being incentivised to work slowly.

Perhaps, if you let your staff go home early if they've completed their work for the day, you might find they start to work more efficiently. You might then be able to gradually increase the work they're asked to do. So long as they've got that chance to go home early, they've got an incentive to work efficiently.

Unfortunately, many firms are plagued by accountancy-types who would be appalled by the idea of people going home early, yet still being paid. They would consider it a waste of money. They would probably have no idea why stopping this practice might drastically reduce efficiency rather than improve it. That's why these decisions should be left, not in the hand of accountants, but in the hands of people who actually understand Economics.

As another example of incentives at work, suppose you run a government department and you ask your staff to find ways that they can work more efficiently. How often do these efficiency drives actually result in greater efficiencies? Hardly ever - but is that surprising? Your staff have got no reason to cooperate with your efficiency drive. If they find ways to work more efficiently, some of them might not be needed anymore and they'll be out of a job. Perhaps, if you told staff that any future pay rises would have to be funded by cutting staff levels, they'd have an incentive to help you find efficiency improvements.

Often, when businesses want to incentivise their staff to work harder or to work more efficiently, they offer managers bonus payments when certain targets are met. The trouble here is that managers often find ways to fiddle the statistics and reach their statistical targets without actually having to do a better job.

For example, managers in hospitals have sometimes been offered bonuses if they could reduce waiting times for patients to have an operation. This was supposed to encourage the managers to find efficiency improvements. Naturally, what a lot of managers did, however, was to cheat. They simply made patients wait longer to see a specialist, since they had to see a specialist before they could actually go on the waiting list for an operation in the first place. The statistical targets were reached and the bonuses were paid, but patients were waiting longer than ever to get their operations.

Often, successfully incentivising people to do a good job is not a crude matter of money - of wages, targets and bonuses. Often, people are much more effectively incentivised simply by their employer trusting them, giving them more freedom and generally just treating them in a decent, respectful way - by treating them as human beings rather than as mere economic units in a production system. Then they might be incentivised to do a good job simply for the job satisfaction they might get from doing things well.

Capital

If you want to produce a product - it could be a car or a simple chocolate bunny - there are many things you are going to need in order to get the job done. These 'things' are often divided into three broad categories - Land, Labour and Capital. These are known as the 'factors of production.'

'Land' essentially refers to all natural resources. 'Labour' refers to people, whether they are workers or managers. Capital, however, is not why you might think. It's not money! 'Capital' actually refers to the man-made things that aid in the production process. It could refer to something as simple as a hammer or a screwdriver - or it could refer to a huge factory.

If this sounds a bit Business-Studies-like - just making up terms for things to make ourselves sound clever - it's actually much more important than that. You see, what's particularly useful about this system of categorising the factors of production, is that it highlights the special nature and importance of capital and the role of capital in determining the economic welfare of our entire society.

Here's the critical thing: We can, in theory, increase the 'land' resources available to us. We could, for example, invade France. Or, we might search for and discover oil. Often, however, we're rather restricted in what we can do to gain more 'land' without taking it away from other people. Even if we discover and make use of a new oil field, we are effectively taking those resources away from future generations.

We can increase the amount of labour available to us. We can encourage people to have more babies, but that might not increase the actual workforce for 18 years or more. We could encourage immigration - but having a more crowded country may bring more problems than benefits.

So, our options in terms of boosting the availability of land and labour can often be rather limited. Capital, however, is something we can really do something very substantial about. We can build new factories so that next year, we are able to build products we weren't able to build this year. We can build better transport systems, so that, next year, people waste less time sitting in traffic jams. We can build new laboratory facilities, so that next year we make more new scientific discoveries than we made this year.

Perhaps, most importantly of all, we can increase our stock of human capital. 'Human capital' refers to the skills, knowledge and understanding that people have build up through education, training and experience. These are, in a sense, 'man-made,' as they were produced by teachers and trainers and by the efforts of their students and trainees - and you end up with 'man-made' skills, knowledge and understanding that aids in the production process and in future scientific and technological achievements. Increasing and improving our capital stock is an area where we can make a huge and lasting difference to the welfare of our society.

The act of increasing our stock of capital, whether this involves building roads, laying new fibre-optic cables for faster internet access or educating our children, is referred to simply as, 'investment.'

Investment

Turn on the news or read a newspaper or look at the news stories on the internet and you'll quickly get the impression that our society is constantly battling economic problems of one kind or another. If we're not in a recession or threatened by recession, then there's a problem with inflation or a budget deficit or a problem with youth unemployment. Sometimes, a whole bunch of problems seem to be occurring at the same time.

Politicians keep promising to get the economy working properly but, unless you've been hiding in a cave for most of your life or are astronomically naive, you're realise that most politicians are actually almost entirely clueless as to how this can be achieved.

So, what is the secret of economic success? How can we all be immensely wealthy and incredibly well-off? There are many people - especially politicians - who like to propagate the idea that even we economists don't know the answer to these questions. This, however, is a blatant lie! Any competent economist knows the answer. It is a simple answer - it's just that politicians and many ordinary people just don't want to listen to it.

I'm now going to tell you something which may come as rather a shock and which appears to run clean counter to the impression given by journalists and politicians alike. The secrets to economic success are not really mysterious or even remotely difficult to understand. There is, in fact, a very straightforward and obvious way to provide for immense economic success. This incredible weapon is known simply as, 'investment.'

The concept of investment is very simple. Each year, we use our resources to provide essential products and services. We need clean water, we need food and we need shelter. Once we've provided for our essential needs, we still have lots of available resources left over. We could use all these resources to have a good time now. Or, we could use at least some of our spare resources to build a better tomorrow. In other words, we can consume our spare resources or we can invest them for the future.

Imagine a simple society from hundreds of years ago where villagers toil all day in the fields in order to scrape together enough to eat. If, by working hard all year, they manage to build up some stocks of food and drink, they could afford to take a few days off. Perhaps they could throw a little party - eat, drink and be merry until their supplies run out. It'll be fun for a few days, but next year they'll be no better off than they were this year.

Alternatively, they could use this opportunity to make some better tools, build some extra carts or bring some extra land under cultivation. Having 'invested' their time and efforts in this way, their work will be easier next year and they'll have a bigger surplus. Then they'll be able to afford to have a party *and* invest further for the future. The next year they'll be even better off - and so on! It's that simple!

You'll notice that this sort of 'investment' doesn't refer to 'investing' money. This sort of investment is far more important than that. This is real investment - the investment of real resources. When people today talk about 'investment,' they're generally referring to 'investing' their money - putting their money into a bank, perhaps, in the hope of receiving interest payments. When proper economists talk about investment, however, they're referring to something much more important - the allocation/investment of real resources to provide such things as capital equipment and infrastructure. We might also be referring to investments in people's skills, improving our scientific understanding and advancing our technology.

If we want to be better off in future, the answer is simple: Waste fewer resources on present-day consumption and devote more resources to improving our infrastructure, updating our stock of capital equipment, improving our technology and educating our people. Then, each year, we can be better off than the year before. Use too many resources on excessive consumption, and we can easily become worse off with each year that goes by.

We just need to put enough resources aside so that our roads, railways, factories and houses are in a better condition at the end of each year than they were at the start. If we cut back on maintaining and upgrading our facilities, equipment and technology, then we've only got our stupid selves to blame if we find ourselves getting worse off rather than better off!

Boom and Bust

Despite Economics being a subject that spans a great many different issues, there is one particular issue that almost totally dominates the economic news and which so concerns politicians and journalists that other - often far more important - economic issues are often swept aside or go unnoticed. That issue is the problem of 'boom and bust.'

Individual economies and the world economy in general tends to go through fairly regular cycles, with periods of 'economic growth' interspersed with periods of recession. This is the economic cycle of 'boom and bust' that we've all become used to and which many people - in politics and in the media - appear to be rather obsessed with.

During the boom years, many businesses appear to be expanding and making decent profits. Production levels increase, unemployment tends to fall and people's wages often go up. Then, there may come a period of recession, when lots of businesses see falling sales, some businesses go bust altogether and unemployment rises.

Read, listen to or watch the news and it always seems as if we are either struggling desperately to avoid an impending recession or struggling desperately to come out of one.

What most obsesses politicians and journalists is a single economic statistic; Gross Domestic Product - usually referred to simply as, 'GDP.' More specifically, it is the rate at which GDP is growing that seems to be of most concern.

In simple terms, GDP is a measure of how much 'economic activity' takes place in an economy (e.g. The US or the UK) in a single year. When goods are being manufactured or services are being provided, this is counted as economic activity. The greater the value of the goods and services that are being produced or provided in a year, the higher GDP will be.

If GDP is increasing by a significant amount, we call this 'economic growth' and members of the government pat themselves on the back for a job well done. As a rough idea, in most years, in most western countries, the government would be satisfied with growth of two percent and absolutely delighted with anything much more than that. On the other hand, any periods of zero growth or 'negative growth' (when GDP actually falls) are a major embarrassment.

A period when GDP is falling might be referred to as a recession, although, these days, it is usually only officially counted as a recession if there are two consecutive three-month periods when GDP falls. We don't generally consider ourselves to have recovered from a recession until we return to a period of significant growth in GDP.

Recessions, of course, are obviously painful, especially for people who lose their jobs or whose businesses go bust. It is important to remember, however, that 'busts' do have an important function. Recessions are important times of change. In order to prosper and to meet our changing needs and wants, the economy needs to change and adapt.

If a business is no longer producing goods we really want or is no longer producing things efficiently, then perhaps it should go bust. When a business goes bust, its shops or industrial units become available for new businesses to start up or for other businesses to expand. Its workers may become unemployed, but this also makes them available to be employed elsewhere. The demise of one business is an opportunity for a new one to grow and expand. If we don't allow a failing business to go bust, then it will continue to hog valuable resources and premises that could have been put to better use by someone else.

A recession is a challenging time when revenues are squeezed and firms are tested to see how robust they are. Recessions, therefore, can be an important catalyst for change - change that may, in time, bring considerable benefits. Resources that are being poorly utilized should be transferred to people or businesses that can put them to better use. People may need to be moved from where they are not being very productive to where they can be more productive.

Recessions, of course, aren't always fair. Sometimes, businesses with a lot of potential get caught out in recessions and go bust, whilst some firms we'd be better off without manage to survive. Nevertheless, this doesn't mean we'd be better off overall without recessions - so perhaps we shouldn't fret quite so much when we have one occasionally. Painful as they usually are, we might end up worse off if we never had any recessions at all.

What might actually be a much bigger problem in the long run than boom and bust, however, is our obsession with boom and bust. The economic news (and, very often, political news) is dominated by the subject of economic growth. Are we staying in recession? Are we heading for recovery? As soon as we're out of one recession, we're scanning for signs of the next one or worrying about whether growth will be as high as predicted or hoped for.

All this talk about economic growth might be what obsesses ignorant politicians and lazy journalists. Any decent economist, however, would question whether this obsession with growth actually makes any sense. They understand perfectly well that economic growth is very far from being the be-all-and-end-all of economic success.

For a start, GDP is only a rather crude and inaccurate measure of economic activity. A lot of activities that are included in GDP statistics aren't actually activities that make us better off. The production and sale of cigarettes, for example, contributes to GDP, but this makes us worse off, not better off.

Then there's the well-known broken window example. If GDP is so important, then why don't we encourage yobs to go around throwing stones and breaking windows? After all, a lot of people would have to be employed fixing those windows and the work they do would contribute towards GDP. Obviously, however, this cycle of destruction and repair wouldn't actually be making us better off. We'd simply be working harder in order to stand still. We'd be better off if the windows didn't get broken in the first place - but that wouldn't boost our GDP statistics!

The importance of GDP is also lessened by the fact that a lot of important economic activity isn't included in GDP statistics. If you pay a babysitter to look after your children, this counts towards GDP, but when Grandma does the babysitting for free, this doesn't count, as there is no record of any transaction having taken place.

The key point overall, however, is the fact that, for a country that is already rich, there is no clear relationship between GDP and how well-off people are. GDP is a very useful statistic when looking at developing countries as they develop from subsistence economies to modern economies, but for modern, rich, western countries, it is far less useful.

In a country like the UK or the US, we're already producing and consuming plenty enough to make ourselves very rich and very well off. Yet, politicians and journalists seem to think that we should strive to produce and consume ever more and more goods and services without end. They act as if it will be disastrous if we don't constantly accelerate the rate at which we are producing and consuming things. But can this acceleration really continue for ever and ever? Even if it can, would we want it to? Would it actually do us any good?

Take a step back and you'll realise that, whatever economic problems we might have, a failure to produce and consume enough things is not one of them. Of course, we still have shortages in some areas and we could do with more of certain products and services and with some goods and services being of a much higher quality, but in terms of the sheer bulk of what we produce and consume - no, there's no shortage there!

No, this obsession with GDP makes no economic sense - and yet it continues. And this obsession itself causes many problems. Our obsession with boom and bust distracts us from what are actually far more important, underlying, economic problems and opportunities.

What about feeding the poor? What about eradicating easily-preventable diseases? What about protecting and preserving wildlife species and habitats? What about educating our populations by addressing the appalling

79

inadequacies in our education systems? Oops - we appear to be too busy worrying about boom and bust to care about these things!

Boom and bust dominate the economics news, but there is so much more to Economics than the economics of boom and bust!

Means and Ends

A lot of economic activity is not an end or an achievement in itself - it is a means rather than an ends.

We build cars and fill them with fuel. This, however, is not, in itself, much of an achievement. The achievement comes when we do something valuable with that car and that fuel. You might use that car to get to work - but that still isn't a meaningful achievement. Whether you achieve something will depend on what you do at work.

Suppose you use your car to get to the factory where you work making computers. Still, we haven't really achieved anything. Whether we've achieved anything will depend on what those computers are used for.

Suppose that some of those computers are used in a marketing department for a cola company. Still we haven't achieved anything. Even if that marketing department successfully manages to convince some people to buy their cola, we've probably achieved nothing of any real economic worth, because the consumers of the cola would probably have been better off drinking water anyway.

Suppose, however, that some of the computers you made are used by the design department of a toy company. They use them to design some toys that eventually get played with by children. The children enjoy playing with those toys. Perhaps now we have actually achieved something worthwhile. A child's enjoyment doesn't have to be justified by what it will lead to or result in - it may be considered to be a positive result in itself.

However, we would then have to look at the huge

resources that went into developing, manufacturing and distributing that toy - and ask if those resources could actually have been used in a different way and produced even more enjoyment as a result.

For example, there would be a lot of parents involved in the production process of a toy - either designing and making the toy itself, or building and maintaining the factory it was made in, or making the computers or machinery that are used in the factory and its offices - and so on. Perhaps we could have brought a great deal more enjoyment and benefit if those parents had simply stayed at home and spent time with their own children.

So, it is important to repeatedly remind ourselves that a lot of 'economic activity' simply enables other economic activity to take place, but does not, in itself, produce any real achievement - and may well not, in the end, even so much as contribute to any real achievement.

In addition, a lot of the 'economic activity' our politicians rejoice in is actually just maintenance activity. It is about maintaining our infrastructure, maintaining our equipment and maintaining the skills of the population. It is about standing still rather than getting anywhere. Roads are mended and cars are serviced. These may be important tasks, but they are 'standing still activities.' They just keep us where we are. This doesn't mean this activity is wasteful activity, but it is only really useful if these maintenance activities do eventually lead to something important actually being achieved.

In order to judge the value of an activity, it makes sense to ask what that activity was or is supposed to achieve. What was the ultimate objective? So, what is all our production leading to? What should it be leading to? What is the point of it all? This is where we could go off into a long debate as to the meaning of life. Should we be seeking scientific advancement, to do good deeds or just to have a good time?

Clearly, we're not likely to all be able to agree on what the ultimate purpose of all our work is supposed to be - it will be different things to different people - but surely we ought to be achieving something? We shouldn't just be blindly making one thing so that that thing can help us make something else which helps us make other things and so on. What is to be the end product of all our rushing around?

The trouble is that, in our constant mithering about the state of the economy, it can be easy to forget that the economy is supposed to be achieving things - achieving various things that we, collectively and individually, consider to be important and of value.

We spend vast amounts of energy supposedly trying to measure the value of all our economic activity. We then spend even more energy obsessing about the statistics we produce as a result. Yet, how can we meaningfully measure the value of all our economic activity if we haven't thought about what all this activity is supposed to achieve?

Mankind is a remarkable species and has achieved many great things. We have learnt to fly, split the atom, begun to unravel the secrets of evolution and genetics, travelled to the moon and created music of a standard that would possibly impress even the most advanced alien species.

There is, however, so much more left still to

achieve. There are many huge problems and great challenges that lie before us. We have poverty and disease to eradicate. We have to learn to look after the planet we live on. There is so much more we can learn about science and technology and art. There's a lot of space to explore. Rather pathetically, we haven't set foot on another planet yet, despite having Mars so conveniently near by!

Taking on many of these great challenges often comes down, essentially, to a problem of resource allocation. To get great things done, sufficient amounts of the right resources have to be allocated to the cause. Today's scientific advancements are the cumulative result of hundreds of years of studying and research by many millions of people - not just in science itself, but in developing advanced communication systems, such as the English language.

The advancement of mankind is, in one sense, a great project in resource-management - and when resources are wasted on things that do nothing to advance mankind, that is a great missed opportunity. If we waste our resources and fail to allocate them wisely, the advancement of mankind will be slowed or brought to a halt. Indeed, our society might even regress if we don't allocate enough resources to advancing or even just maintaining it. Some people would even argue that this is already happening - as we waste our time and resources chasing empty dreams of economic growth with no purpose.

It is a very fashionable disease - especially amongst politicians - to obsess about economic activity for economic activity's sake, without ever really stopping to properly consider what all this economic activity is supposed to achieve. People with this disease fail to distinguish between means and ends, get confused and start regarding means as ends in themselves. It is the job of a skilled economist to be constantly aware of this error, to avoid it and to encourage other people to avoid it. We can then concentrate more of our efforts on actually achieving things of real value.

My Website:

To find out more about my work, including my other books, please visit **www.IMOS.org.uk**

Your comments on this book are welcome at: Rob@IMOS.org.uk

Some of my other books:

Here is Wosdom
Seeking Wosdom
Pearls of Wosdom
An Intelligent Life
Gifted
Whatever Happened to the Life of Leisure?
The Education of a Poker Player
Revelations: An Intelligent Analysis of Religious Beliefs

Printed in Great Britain
by Amazon